Wil

Roy Williams, OBE, worke... ... ...actor before turning writing full-time in 1990. He g............ .... Rose Bruford in 1995 with a first-class BA Honours degree in Writing, and participated in the 1997 Carlton Television screenwriters' course. *The No Boys Cricket Club* (1996) won him nominations for the TAPS Writer of the Year Award 1996 and for the Writers' Guild of Great Britain New Writer of the Year Award 1996. He was the first recipient of the Alfred Fagon Award 1997 for *Starstruck* (1998), which also won the 31st John Whiting Award and the EMMA Award 1999. *Lift Off* (1999) was the joint winner of the George Devine Award 2000. His other plays include *Night and Day* (1996); *Josie's Boys* (1996); *Souls* (1999); *Local Boy* (2000); *The Gift* (2000); *Clubland* (Royal Court, 2001), winner of the *Evening Standard* Charles Wintour Award for the Most Promising Playwright; *Fallout* (2003); *Sing Yer Heart Out for the Lads* (2002); *Little Sweet Thing* (2005); *Slow Time* (2005); *Days of Significance* (2007); *Absolute Beginners* (2007); *Joe Guy* (2007); *Baby Girl* (2007); *Out of the Fog* (2007); *There's Only One Wayne Matthews* (2007); *Category B* (2009); *Sucker Punch* (2010); an adaptation of *The Loneliness of the Long-Distance Runner* (2012); *Advice for the Young at Heart* (2013); *Kingston 14* (2014) and *Antigone* (2014). He was awarded the OBE for Services to Drama in the 2008 Birthday Honours List.

Roy Williams

Wildefire

Bloomsbury Methuen Drama
An imprint of Bloomsbury Publishing Plc

BLOOMSBURY
LONDON · NEW DELHI · NEW YORK · SYDNEY

Bloomsbury Methuen Drama

An imprint of Bloomsbury Publishing Plc

Imprint previously known as Methuen Drama

50 Bedford Square	1385 Broadway
London	New York
WC1B 3DP	NY 10018
UK	USA

www.bloomsbury.com

BLOOMSBURY, METHUEN DRAMA and the Diana logo
are trademarks of Bloomsbury Publishing Plc

First published 2015

© Roy Williams, 2015

British Library Cataloguing-in-Publication Data
A catalogue record for this book is available from the British Library

ISBN: PB: 978-1-4742-3611-9
ePDF: 4742-3613-3
ePub: 978-1-4742-3612-6

Library of Congress Cataloging-in-Publication Data
A catalog record for this book is available from the Library of Congress

Typeset by Country Setting, Kingsdown, Kent CT14 8ES

Wildefire received its world premiere at the Hampstead Theatre on 6 November 2014. The cast was as follows:

Lee	Eric Kofi Abrefa
Vince/Lukas	Cian Barry
Spence	Ricky Champ
Sean	Danny Dalton
Marcus/Officer	Sammy Hayman
Kristal	Tara Hodge
Don	Fraser James
Chris	Simon Manyonda
Kid/Merchant	Noof Ousellam
Gail	Lorraine Stanley
Maxine	Sharlene Whyte

Director   Maria Aberg
Designer   Naomi Dawson
Lighting   James Farncombe
Movement   Ayse Tashkiran
Sound   Gareth Fry
Fight Director   Kate Waters

Wildefire

Characters

Gail, *mid to late thirties. She lives up to her surname, is 'wild' and full of 'fire'. Extremely tough, and very brave. Good sense of humour, but can be stubborn, defensive and lash out. In denial about her addiction to painkillers.*

Don, *early forties. Loyal, dependable, a born leader, but has a temper which has become shorter with age. Is becoming jaded and tired of his life as a police officer.*

Spence, *late thirties. Quick witted, life and soul of any party, also dependable, but can be impatient and judgemental.*

Maxine, *early forties. Loud and raucous, but was once a good copper. She can be sympathetic and caring, a big sister to everyone. Now bitter and angry towards the police.*

Vince, *mid twenties. Young, ambitious, committed, but can be naive. He believes he is not as innocent or as self-righteous as he looks, and hates it when others think he is: hence the slight chip on his shoulder.*

Chris, *early twenties. Too cocky for his own good and beginning to realise that. He is always eager to prove himself.*

Kristal, *white, twenties.*

Lee, *any race, late teens.*

Marcus, *white, twenties.*

Officer, *white, late thirties.*

Lukas, *white, late twenties.*

Sean, *white, late thirties.*

Peel, *white, forties.*

Kid, *any race, nineteen.*

Merchant, *any race, twenties.*

Possible doubling

Sean and Peel, Merchant and Kid, Vince and Lukas, Officer and Marcus.

Setting

Various locations around South London including a police station.

Act One

Lights on **Sir Robert Peel**. *He looks extremely well-presented in period dress as he addresses Parliament.*

Peel   Mr Speaker, it will be my profound pleasure to call upon the attention of the House the following nine principles which will be set out as general instructions issued to every new police officer in our new Metropolitan Police Force.

To prevent crime and disorder, as an alternative to their repression by military force and severity of legal punishment.

To recognise always that the power of the police to fulfil their functions and duties is dependent on public approval of their existence, actions and behaviour and on their ability to secure and maintain public respect.

To recognise always that to secure and maintain the respect and approval of the public means also the securing of the willing co-operation of the public in the task of securing observance of laws.

To recognise always that the extent to which the co-operation of the public can be secured diminishes proportionately the necessity of the use of physical force and compulsion for achieving police objectives.

To seek and preserve public favour, by ready offering of individual service and friendship to all members of the public without regard to their wealth or social standing.

To use physical force only when the exercise of persuasion, advice and warning is found to be to obtain public co-operation to an extent necessary to secure observance of law.

To recognise always the need for strict adherence to police executive functions, and to refrain from even seeming to usurp the powers of the judiciary of avenging individuals or the State.

To recognise always that the test of police efficiency is the absence of crime and disorder and not the visible evidence of police action in dealing with them.

And finally, to maintain at all times a relationship with the public that gives reality to the historic tradition, that the police are the public and that the public are the police.

Present day.

A police station somewhere in South London. It is complete mayhem. The entire relief is bringing in a crowd of drunken football hooligans. Some are wearing Millwall shirts, the others are wearing Charlton shirts, but they are all hurling abuse at each other. **Don** *can barely hear himself speak.*

Gail *enters, dressed in full uniform. It is her first day, she looks a little disorientated as all of this is going on around her.*

Don   I know Millwall lost 4–1 today, but this taking it a bit far, isn't it?

Right, I want all of Charlton Athletic in cells, there, eight and ten. Millwall can have nine, five and six, and unless you want to be cleaning claret off the walls for the next month, I suggest no mix-ups. (*Yells.*) Will you all please just shut up!

The hooligans turn the volume down.

Don   Thank you. Let's have them one by one. Christopher?

Chris *brings the first hooligan to the desk as the others line up behind.*

Don   Name, age, address, and do not even think of pissing me about!

The hooligan throws up all over the front desk.

Chris   Oh, you bastard! Slag!

Don   Cells, now!

Chris *throws the hooligan to a couple of colleagues who round the hooligans up and usher them off towards the cells.*

Don   You're cleaning this up.

Chris   Fuck off, am I!

Don   It's 'Fuck off, am I, Sarge', and don't give me no lip.

Chris   Jesus, it stinks.

Don   No shit, find a bucket.

Chris   I'm not touching that.

Don   You get a sponge or a cloth, you dosey waz!

Gail   Excuse me?

Don   I'm breathing it in, Chris, I am not happy.

Chris   Yeah, but where . . .

Don   Just look.

Gail   Excuse me?

Don   Yes, love, what?

Gail   It might be a good idea to remove any solid pieces of the vomit with a paper towel.

Chris   Fuck that.

Gail   Do you have a cat?

Don   What?

Gail   A station cat?

Don   No. We do not have a station cat.

Gail   That's a shame.

Don   And why is that?

Gail   Cat litter is really good to sprinkle over the liquid, it forms a solid mass then, quite quickly. The liquid, that is. Baking soda will do it, just as well.

Don   Who are you?

Gail   Sorry, I'm Wilde.

Don   Oh, are you now?

Gail   Gail Wilde. Transfer from Horsham.

Don   Yes. I know who you are, Wilde.

Gail   Call me Gail.

Don   Call me Sarge.

Gail   Yes, Sarge.

Don (*sees she is already in uniform*)   You're eager.

Gail   Not really, just keen to get started.

Don   Canteen is through the door on your left, locker room on the right, parade begins in five minutes, and don't you ever think about being late.

Gail   No worry. About me being late I mean, because I won't be. Not ever.

Don   Glad to hear, off you pop.

Gail   I'm really glad to be here, Sarge.

Don   You'll learn.

Gail *goes.*

Don *sees that* **Chris** *is still there, staring at* **Gail** *as she leaves.*

Don   Chris, why are you still here?

Chris   Wildefire!

Don   Is there more to that?

Chris   Gail Wildefire, that's what we called her. We were at Hendon the same time. The boys and me used to watch her through the window when she was working out in the gym. Nice quads. And don't get me started when she used to wear shorts, do you know what I mean?

Don   Bucket. Baking soda. You. Find. Now!

Spence *comes in.*

Spence (*chants*)   4–1! 4–1! 4–1! 4–1! . . .

Don   Leave it, Spence, just leave it!

Spence   You wish, mate.

Don   Penalty my arse! No way was that a penalty! No way!

Spence   You lot, with yer Arsenal and Chelsea, when are you going to understand, Charlton Athletic are kings and will always be kings.

Don   Do you have any idea what that Number Nine of yours has cost me? Do yer? Stevie Wonder could have seen that was a dive.

Spence   Maybe you should stick with the horses, eh, Sarge?

Don   Maybe I should give you a slap? Eh, Spence?

Spence   Right. Where's the new boy?

Chris   Girl actually. And wait until you see it, mate.

Don   'It', Constable?

Chris (*aside*)   Oh yeah, here we go.

Don   Did I hear you refer one of your colleagues, who may end up watching your back one day, as an *it*?

Chris   Absolutely not, Sarge, you know me better than that. I have nothing but respect for my fellow officer of the law. Irrespective of age, gender, class or race. (*Aside.*) My batty hole!

Don   Oi! (*To* **Spence**.) How's your slag doing?

Spence   I left him in his cell last night, shitting his pants.

Chris   So, that's what it was.

Spence   One more push after parade should do it. By the way, I need another body in there with me, Manning is giving evidence in court this morning. Fancy it, Chris?

Chris   On it, bruv!

Don 'On it, bruv'? Don't talk in here, like you do out there.

Chris Sorry, Dad.

Don Stand fast, Constable. (*To* **Spence**.) Take in the new girl.

Chris See if she likes it on top.

Don Christopher, *don't make me angry.*

Chris Alright, I'm going.

Don Because you wouldn't like me when I'm angry,

Chris My legs. They are moving. See?

He goes.

Spence When's your interview?

Don This afternoon. You're in charge.

Spence Nervous?

Don Fuck off, am I?

Spence (*excited*) Nearly there, mate.

Don (*more excited*) Nearly there, Spence!

They high-five each other.

Spence 'Inspector Walters!' Eh?

Don Nice, ring to it, don't you think?

Spence Better believe.

Don Don't kiss my arse just yet. We have the worst stats for violent crime this side of the river, Spence. This whole nick needs some serious cleaning up.

Spence And you're the man to do it.

Don I've got serious intel coming in that's going to put me well over the finishing line.

Spence Care to share?

Don   All in good time, Spencer.

Gail *brings in a nervous looking young suspect into the interview room and sits him down.* **Spence** *joins* **Gail** *as they face the scared-looking* **Kid**.

Spence   Look at me, son, come on, look at me. We can sort this out. Are you with me?

The **Kid** *nods.*

Spence   Right then, I have been reading up on you. You have come a long way from school, haven't you? I bet you wish you were still there now. Dropping out at sixteen because you had a hard-on this big to play the bad man, what was that about? Where did you think you would be when you turned eighteen, in a penthouse? I need you to tell me about the rape? What was it, an initiation? 'Do this ting, you join the crew', is that how it go?

Door knocks. **Chris** *enters.*

Chris   Spence, do you have a minute?

Gail *(to the tape)*   PC Liburd has entered the room.

Chris   Sorry, I need a signature. ID parade. The OAP who was mugged in the park.

Spence *signs the form.*

Chris *goes.*

Gail *(to the tape)*   PC Liburd has left the room.

The **Kid** *shuffles uncomfortably in his seat.*

Spence   The girl is fifteen years old, did you know that?

Kid   Listen . . .

Spence   No, you listen, just be quiet for a minute, please. What I have to say now is important.

Knock on door. **Chris** *comes in again with another form.*

Chris   Me again, sorry.

Gail   PC Liburd has entered the room.

Chris   I almost forgot. Another ID parade. The King George pub?

Spence *signs the form.*

Chris *leaves.*

Gail   PC Liburd has left the room.

Spence   Fifteen years old, son. Passed around your brers, one by one.

The **Kid** *begins to cry.* **Spence** *hands him a tissue.*

The **Kid** *dries his eyes.*

Spence   You alright? Are you fit to carry on?

The **Kid** *nods.*

Spence   We know you were there. I am not saying, you joined in. Maybe you were the lookout, or maybe you just stood and watched. It's alright to admit you were scared, you're in well over your head. Sometimes trouble finds you. It's hard being young in this city. I have a son your age. Trouble found him. He went off the rails a little, a bit like you. But it is never too late to make things good. It all starts with one small decision. He's off to university now. He won. He chose who he wanted to be. I couldn't be more proud. This is your decision. Your big choice. And I want to help you.

Door knocks. It is **Chris** *again with another form.*

Chris   Mate, I'm really sorry to keep doing this to you.

Spence   What?!

Gail   PC Liburd has entered the room.

Spence   Jesus Christ, are you on commission or something? How many Roasts have you've got today?

Chris   Six actually, plus three outstanding from yesterday.

Spence   Yes, alright.

Chris   Clint is still on the computer with his witness – that phone shop robbery.

Spence   Well, use the other one then.

Chris   Other one is down.

Spence   What, again?

Chris   No, not again, still! And we are waiting for that IT bloke to come and fix it.

Spence   Am I the only senior officer in this nick right now?

Chris   Harris is off sick. Manning is giving evidence in court. The skipper is at Scotland Yard for his interview. I'm getting nothing but blank looks from what is left of CID.

Spence   All right, all right, all right, just shut up.

Spence *signs the form.*

Spence   And tell Clint to hurry it up.

Chris   I shall not be bothering you again.

Chris *goes.*

Gail   PC Liburd has left the room.

Spence   Will you please stop that? Give me the names of the other boys, son. I know you know them. Tell me who they are, they will never know we heard it from you and you can walk away from this, get on with your life, go back to school if you fancy, make your mum and dad proud, or you can choose to spend the rest of your life knowing that you chose to be this little girl's nightmare. I know what you want to do. I'm just wondering if you're brave enough.

He hands him pen and paper. The suspect writes the names.

Ah, you see, there you go. You are making me feel proud already.

Gail *and* **Spence** *walk straight into the next scene, having a drink with* **Spence**, **Maxine** *and* **Chris**.

Chris   I don't know why you continue to have the arsehole about it.

Spence   You wouldn't listen.

Chris   Oh, here we go.

Spence   Would you fucking listen?

Chris   What was the problem?

Spence   Gail, you're new, you be the judge. Listen up.

Gail   I'm listening.

Spence   Chris and I got this call-out. Some Chinese bloke, I can't remember his name.

Chris   Just call him Wong for now.

Maxine   Oh, that's original.

Chris   What are you, Max, the Chinese surname police?

Spence   Oi, my wife, behave. Where was I?

Gail   Wong?

Spence   Right, this Wong, he's on his way home from work, gets jumped, and mugged, nasty! They pulled him to the floor, kicked him around a little and made off with his hard-earned cash. Take the money, I understand, but kick him? A seventy-year-old man? I mean, where's the sense?

Chris   You're drifting.

Spence   No, I'm not. Good news though was that this slag had done it before, even better, we had a witness. We found the slag quite quick and took him in and it was everything in me then not to beat him senseless.

Chris   And then?

Spence   And then Chris here takes Mister Wong's address to pick him up for the ID parade. Imagine his shock as well as his delight to find Mister Wong ran a Chinese takeaway along with his wife and eight kids.

Spence   Eight!

Maxine   Is that relevant, babe?

Spence   Just saying.

Chris   Their specialty, Gail, kung pao chicken!

Spence   Died and gone to heaven were his next thoughts.

Chris   You are not *wong*!

Spence   When he brought Wong back home, he must have some sixth sense on him, because he knew straight off Chinese grub was Chris's thing.

Chris   He didn't know, how could he know?

Spence   Do you mind, I'm telling the story here.

Chris   Well, tell it right then.

Spence   He offered him a takeaway free of charge. The next evening, Christopher just happened to be walking, getting the train home, when Mister Wong sees him from across the road, waves to him, offers him another free bag of his very delicious kung pao! (*To* **Chris**.) Is that right enough for you?

Chris   You may continue.

Spence   The next day, moron here takes a right liberty.

Chris   I just wanted to know if it would work.

Spence   He goes out of his way to make sure he was on the right side of Mister Wong's takeaway, so he could see him from the winder. Sure enough, he did. Waves him in, another bag sorted for the night. Now, this is where you come in, Gail. Tell me, what is wrong with this picture?

Gail   I suppose it could be misconstrued as accepting a bribe.

Spence   Thank you, the prosecution rests.

Chris   Bollocks.

Maxine   What's bollocks, you sap?

Chris   Free food, that is all it was.

Spence   Oh, help me someone!

Gail   Any such recompense could lead you to facing charges of bribery and corruption.

Chris   Jesus wept!

Maxine   So, for your sake as well as your heart, Chris, learn how to peel a potato, you stupid cunt.

Gail *is a little startled to hear* **Maxine** *use the word.*

Chris   See what you have walked in on, Wildefire?

Gail   Hendon, right? I thought you looked familiar.

Chris   The boys and me used to talk about you.

Spence   Oi! That's another level, Chris.

Gail   That's all you boys could do, talk! I see nothing has changed.

Chris   Well, sorry if my conversation skills are not up to standard.

Maxine   So, what's your story then, Gail, what are you doing here? Why this job?

Gail   My grandad was in uniform. He was stationed at Mile End. He used to tell me stories.

Maxine   Like what? What stories?

Gail   Well, like he would say, if he caught a kid pinching out of the sweetshop, instead of nicking the kid, he would buy the sweets for them, out of his own pocket, but only as long as they gave the sweets back first, and say they were sorry.

Maxine   Little bit more to it now, I think.

Gail   I know that, I just liked the simplicity of it. It was all about crime prevention with him. He had a lot of respect. The whole of Mile End showed up for his funeral.

Maxine   How sweet?

Gail   What's the matter with that?

Spence   Not a thing, Gail.

Gail   Listen, I've been meaning to say, Spence, that was a really good interview with that kid by the way. Bloody great in fact. You had him right here.

Maxine   Yes girl, make him blush.

Gail   It was you talking about your son is what did it, I think.

Maxine   Son?

Gail   Going to university, making you proud.

Spence   The closest he is has ever got to university, Gail, is when he passes it on his way to the job centre.

Maxine   So, how did you find your first day then?

Gail   Not bad.

Spence   Horsham it ain't though, right?

Gail   Horsham had its moments as well, you know.

Max   Oh yes, such as?

Gail   Town centre, it wouldn't be a weekend without a ruck.

Max   Oh did you hear that, Spence? It wouldn't be the weekend without a ruck.

Gail   My very first day on the job, I got into it with someone.

Max   Well, let's hear it.

Chris   Drum roll.

Gail   Barely an hour in when I was called a fat ugly hairy-arms frigid beaver-bumping bitch.

Maxine   Is that it?

Gail   No. We were moving on this drunk from some restaurant, once we got him into the car he took one look at me, and it was a red rag, 'bitch' this, 'whore' that, going into extreme detail about having a cock this big that he wants to shove right into me.

Max   Drunks say a lot of things, it's what they do matters.

Gail   I know that. He was only off his head anyway, he couldn't say sorry enough when he sobered up. I almost felt sorry for him. I'm just saying, Horsham was quiet, but it could be rough.

Chris   Then why leave?

Gail   I wanted to join the Met. I wanted the buzz.

Maxine   I was on the response team during the riots. When our van was surrounded we could hear the pelting from inside. A brick came flying through the back of the van, missing my head by this much. Then this hand came through, waving a machete around, of all things. He caught me on the shoulder.

Spence   That little slag.

Maxine   Is that the kind of buzz you had in mind, Gail?

Gail   Obviously not, Maxine.

Chris   Then get the next train back to Horsham, love. This is the Met!

Gail   I know what it is, and it's 'Gail', in case you didn't hear, not 'love'!

Chris   Alright, Wildefire.

Gail   Will you stop calling me that?

Chris   What is this, are the painters in this week?

Spence   Oh!

Maxine   Out of order, Chris.

Chris   Oh, move!

Maxine (*to* **Gail**)   And you unwind, yeah? We're just getting a feel of you, that's all.

Chris   A good feel!

Gail   Like you would know where it is, Chris.

Spence (*laughs*)   Oi, oi!

Chris   I'm willing to bet yours is like a grapefruit, Gail, squirts when you eat it.

Spence   Oh, you sick man.

Chris (*revelling*)   Have it!

Spence   You are sick.

Gail   You might get a taste one day, if you're lucky!

The officers laugh.

Spence   Go on, Chris, take her up on it.

Chris   Fuck off.

Spence   You're alright, Gail. And that's official.

Chris   And on that note. Another?

Chris *goes inside.*

Spence   Have you ever seen him move so fast?

Maxine   Always happens, when he gets bitch-slapped.

Gail   So, does that mean I can stay?

Maxine   We said you're alright, so relax. You might want to dial it down a little about the grandad talk. When was the last time we were respected? Or cared about, for that matter.

Gail   I think they do care, deep down.

Maxine   Load of bollocks! To them we are nothing but a bunch of racist, sexist, overpaid thugs in uniform.

Gail   And yet you still manage to put that uniform on each morning.

Maxine   Not for long.

Spence   Don't listen to her, Gail.

Maxine   No, do listen to me, Gail.

Gail   Come again?

Maxine   I'm retiring, as of next year. I've done my twenty-five. I'm getting out before they stop us doing that, the bastards. (*To* **Spence**.) You didn't mention?

Spence   Why would I mention it to her?

Maxine   Oh, oh, so she is not here for my benefit then?

Spence   Babe?

Maxine   To remind me what it was like my first day, the buzz?

Spence   You're paranoid.

Maxine   You're transparent. No offence, Gail.

Spence   I brought her to have a drink. First day, get the new boy, or girl, roaring pissed. Peel's tenth point of policing? Not everything is about you, darling.

Maxine   Oh, ouch.

Gail (*feeling awkward*)   Erm, maybe I should . . .

Maxine   Maybe what? Relax.

Spence   You got amongst it during the riots.

Maxine   Oh, Jesus H!

Spence   You stood your ground. What you were paid for, trained for. Some slags give you agg, and you are done?

Maxine   If you had any sense, you would get out as well.

Spence   And do what? And don't tell me about Mark.

Maxine   He's offered me a job now.

Spence   Oh babe, opening doors all day for the public is no job, that's a life sentence.

Maxine   And what do you call this?

Spence   The best that we are.

Maxine   That is such a LOB!

Spence   Me, a security guard? Sitting on my arse, be fat and old before my time. To be invisible to everyone. You might as well kill me.

Maxine (*mocks*)   No buzz!

Spence   That's right! No buzz!

Gail   I think I really should –

Maxine   It's alright, Gail.

Spence (*to* **Gail**)   Just sit down.

Maxine   Well, I'm not you.

Spence   You used to be.

Maxine   You can take this 'buzz' and shove it up your arse.

Spence   There are people you can talk to you, you know that?

Maxine   Oh, for what I hope is the last fucking time, this is not about Croydon! This has nothing to do with the buzz! This has everything to do with you being scared.

Spence   Alright, yeah, I'm scared. That what you want to hear? I'm scared. This is all I know, and it's all you know. No one travels on blues as fast as you do, Max, I can't believe you are turning your back. We do this because we don't know how not to, right or wrong?

Gail *walks into the next scene with* **Kristal**.

Kristal   You're so fucking wrong. Who told you?

Spence *and* **Maxine** *go.*

Gail   A concerned neighbour of yours.

Kristal   Let me guess, that Asian woman from two doors down.

Gail   She sounded worried.

Kristal   Nosey little bitch.

Gail   Come on now. There is no need for that.

Kristal   You are having a go because I say bitch?

Gail   Well, it's not nice, is it? Please, don't say it any more.

Kristal   An argument, that is all he wants.

Gail   What kind of an argument, Ms Turner?

Kristal   We have them all the time, we are a couple.

Gail (*observes* **Kristal**'s *shiner*)   Do you get those bruises on your face all of the time?

Kristal   You should see what I give him.

Gail   I saw him, Ms Turner, kicking and screaming all of the way here. It took four of us to restrain him, but I didn't see any marks on him. Not a single bruise. Marcus must heal quite quickly.

Kristal   There you go. Are you going to let him go now? Come on, man, I have to pick up my little ones from school.

Gail   That's not a worry. I have a car, I can take you if you like?

Kristal   You can be as nice to me all you want.

Gail   I'm just doing my job, Ms Turner. And I care about what happens to you.

Kristal   You don't even know me.

Gail   I still care. Now, if you want, we can do something about this. We can begin with me asking you just a few simple questions.

Kristal   I'm not going to testify.

Gail   About what? You said you fell. That is correct, isn't it, Ms Turner? You can talk to me, darling.

Kristal   I'm not your darling!

Gail   I'm sorry.

Kristal   And I won't make a statement, anything like that.

Gail   You don't have to.

Kristal   Right, so we're done.

Gail   What I mean is, we do not need a statement from you to charge your husband –

Kristal   He's not my husband.

Gail   – if we believe he has committed an assault against you.

Kristal   Which he hasn't.

Gail   That can be enough to charge him, and take him to court.

Kristal   Yes, but would you?

Gail   Do you want us to? Is that what you want? What is it that you want? Kristal? Tell me. Come on, don't be scared.

Kristal   No.

Gail   Ms Turner, please, look at your face.

Kristal   From falling down the stairs, how many more times.

Gail   I am only trying to help. I want to help. You can talk to me.

Kristal   I'm going to keep on saying until you get it – are you getting it?

Gail   I'm getting it, there is no need to shout, please.

Kristal   You wouldn't believe how much of a fuck I do not give.

Gail   And please don't swear at me? Now, Mrs Gupta.

Kristal   Nosey bitch.

Gail   That is not nice and it is not kind. Mrs Gupta said she heard screaming so loud coming from your flat, she was convinced your life was in danger. She also heard sounds that suggested your head was being slammed against the wall.

Kristal   Heard, not seen. Heard! I should be a lawyer. I'd get him off.

Gail   Listen to me, if you are scared –

Kristal   But I ain't scared.

Gail   If *anyone* has been threatening you –

Kristal   Which they are not.

Gail   We can help you. That is all I am saying. (*Scribbles on a piece of paper.*) This is my number. In case you change your mind. We are not all bad, you know.

Kristal *goes to leave, but she comes back and takes* **Gail***'s number.*

Gail *smiles.*

She walks into the next scene with **Spence***.*

A couple of hoodie teenagers look like they are up to no good as they huddle up towards each other. They are in the middle of a minor drug deal. They disperse quickly when they see **Gail** *and* **Spence**.

Spence   Ten things you should never say to a copper, I'll start. 'I pay your wages.' Gail?

Gail   Erm . . .

Spence   Come on, it's easy. All the things you've heard.

Gail   'You're a bit short for a copper.'

Spence   That's it. 'Are you one of the village people?' I bloody hate that one.

Gail   'Yer not gonna check the boot, are yer?'

Spence   'How many white people have you stopped?'

Gail   'If I was speeding, so were you.'

Spence   'You shouldn't have shot that kid.'

Gail   'You are under a vest!'

Spence   'I can smell bacon on you.'

Gail   'If I show you my cock, will you let me off?'

Spence   The perfect ten!

Gail   So, what are we doing here?

Spence   We are on a visit.

Gail   To?

Spence   Lee Parker, aged seventeen. Likes to be called 'Little L'.

Gail   Jay Z wannabe, is he?

Spence   Something like that. Now, I need you to play along.

Gail   With what?

Lee *and his brers enter playing basketball.*

Spence   Just play. (*To the boys.*) Lee Parker? Is there a Lee Parker here? Hello? I said hello? Anyone home?

The boys can hear her, but they ignore them as they continue to play ball.

 Spence   How about Little L?

The boys are continuing to ignore him, some of them are giggling.

Spence (*points to* **Gail**)   You're keeping a lady waiting here, where's your manners? Look, I really don't have time for this.

He interrupts the game and grabs the ball. The boys protest.

Yeah, you're crying now, you shouldn't make it so easy, should you!

Lee   You wanna pass our ball back?

Spence   Please tell me you're Lee?

Lee   Little L.

Spence   It's what I was calling yer, why didn't you answer?

Lee   My business, what you want?

Spence   You can lose the tone for a start. Aren't you forgetting something? Statement? Knife attack, you are due in court.

Lee   Yeah, I know.

Spence   So, where's your statement?

Lee   Look, I made a mistake.

Spence   A mistake?

Lee   I didn't see anything.

Spence   You were the one getting attacked, Lee. You must have seen something.

Lee   I didn't.

Spence   Alright.

Lee   So, we done?

Spence   No, we are not done.

Lee   You can't arrest me.

Spence   Dis bwoi love himself! Because I can. Now, I'm going to ask you one last time: has anyone threatened you?

Lee   Why don't you step? We got a game to finish.

Spence   Why don't you make us?

Gail   Spence?

Spence   I'd pay money to see you try.

Lee   Simple as ABC.

Spence   You what?

Lee   I don't chat to no battyboy feds!

The boys around **Lee** *laugh.* **Spence** *grabs* **Lee** *and holds him up against the wall.*

Spence   Try it, just for me, I'm begging yer.

The boys look menacing as they circle **Gail** *and* **Lee**.

Gail   Alright, boys, let's all take a long deep breath now, shall we? You as well, eh, Spence. Spence?

Spence *loosens his grip on* **Lee**.

Gail   There you see, crisis over. Now, we are just going to have a talk with Lee here, then we will be on our way. Everyone happy? Happy?

The boys retreat, then disperse.

Spence (*impressed*)   Respect and feared, eh? Nice one.

Gail (*appreciated*)   Thanks.

Spence   Keep an eye, in case they come back.

Gail   Right.

Spence *takes* **Lee** *aside.*

Lee   Hey, man, what the fuck?

Spence   I have been leaving messages on your phone for days.

Lee   Yes, and?

Spence   What part of the message that was 'bloody call me' did you not get?

Lee   Shoulda left a text.

Spence   Dozens of them.

Lee   I didn't see them.

Spence   So, I have been wasting my time? Keeping yer arse outta jail and that? You have any idea how much I hate texting, Lee?

Lee (*in fear*)   No.

Spence   I can't fart loud enough, Lee, to tell you how much I hate texting. All that touch screen shit. T becomes 2, H becomes R. But according to you, I have been wasting my time.

Lee   No!

Spence   Wrong! You are so wrong.

Lee   I said no!

Spence   How would you like to me to drive your arse around your endz so that Jermaine and the rest of his brers will find out you is my own personal little bitch?

Lee   Oh, come on, Spence . . .

Spence   Spence now, is it?

Lee   We know you ain't going to do that.

Spence   Why is that?

Lee   They will dead me like that is why.

Spence   Like you is a big man. You seem sure I give a shit.

Lee   What you want tell me?

Spence   Answer your bloody phone for one.

Lee   Done.

Spence   You do for me, not the other way round.

Lee   Done, man!

Spence   Some girl got gang raped on Kingsley Road, did you hear about that? I thought you had Jermaine's ear about keeping a lid on these initiations?

Lee   Jermaine ain't happy about it as well, you know. But you any idea how big his crew is? We got brers I don't know.

Spence   I'll drive you round the endz right now, Lee.

Lee   Spence?

Spence   Sirens blaring.

Lee   Hear me –

Spence   All that!

Lee   You done?

Spence   Ain't lying. (*Grabs him again.*) As God is my witness, Lee, I will fuck you through a wall.

Lee   You don't think you might be losing it a little?

Spence   I said no violence, no rapes.

Lee   Alright, man, I'll have words.

Spence   Do that. Speaking of Jermaine, anything happening on the estate, doing any to-ings and go-ings that we should know about?

Lee   No, it's all quiet.

Spence   As soon as you know, I know, yeah?

Lee   What's the hurry?

Spence   None of your business, just do as you're told.

He stuffs some notes into **Lee**'s *hand.*

Spence   If anyone asks, you were in the cop shop for an hour and a half.

Lee   You think I don't know?

He goes.

Spence   Well, if you are the copper I think you are, PC Wilde, you will know we aren't really on a call-out.

Gail   Right, so he's a grass.

Spence   I prefer the term CHIS!

Gail   Chis?

Spence   'Covert Human Intelligence Source'.

Gail   And is this Covert Human Intelligence Source registered?

Spence   He was, now he isn't.

Gail   That's against procedure.

Spence   No shit.

Gail   I don't know about this.

Spence   Do you know how much money the Met spent on chissys last year? Under two million. Year before that it was over three. Word from the Commissioner himself, no more cash. So excuse me if I choose to go rogue a little. It's my money, my risk.

Gail   Why risk? His gang do rapes!

Spence   Look, violent crime was on the up last year. I'm just doing what I can to get the numbers down. Make us look good, including the skipper. With any luck, he'll be made Inspector and we'll finally have a guvnor who knows his elbow from his arse. Now, is any of that alright with you?

Gail   Of course it is.

Spence   Good man!

Gail   'Man'?

Spence   Everyone's 'man'. Right, let's jog on.

Gail *comes home late.* **Sean** *has waited up for her.*

Gail   Oh no, I'm so sorry.

Sean   It's alright.

Gail   I had meant to leave on time today, I really did. I just didn't think.

Sean   Not a problem.

Gail   Thing is –

Sean   Gail, it's OK.

Gail   It was the end of the shift, they all said, let's go out for a beer, again! I couldn't say no, Sean, could I? I mean, how would it make me look? I've only been there for a week.

Sean   Of course. Who was there?

Gail   Usual. Spence, Maxine, Chris.

Sean   You look tired, babe.

Gail   Am bloody knackered. But first things first. What do you fancy eating? I can make you a nice stir-fry.

Sean   Sounds great.

Gail   Oh, and let me know what shirt you're wearing tomorrow. I'll iron it before I go to bed.

Sean   I'll do it, I can iron my shirt.

Gail   No offence, babe, but you can't. When you iron, you put creases back. It's no worry, I can do it. I got to have my sexy man looking all good for his job interview, haven't I?

Sean   I might not need it.

Gail   Why? How did today's one go?

Sean   Good. Really good. I came away with a really good feeling.

Gail   There, you see, I told you you would get back on your feet, but you never believe me.

Sean   I said I had a good feeling, I didn't say I got the job.

Gail   Of course you are going to get it. I mean, they can't hate you lot for ever, now can they?

Sean   It will be a massive drop in wages.

Gail   We'll manage.

Sean   I'll be earning less than the branch manager.

Gail   I said . . .

Sean   Let me finish. A customer advisor, Gail. I'm right back where I started ten years ago.

Gail   Is that it, are you going to stop crying now?

Sean (*defensive*)   I'm not crying.

Gail   And I'm joking. Ease up. Look, before I left Horsham I put in my application to become Sergeant. I have my first round of interviews within the year, by then I will know this entire endz backwards, be able to tell my slags from my lefties.

Sean   Slags and lefties?

Gail   I will dazzle them all. So smile.

Sean   What's with all this banter you are bringing back?

Gail   I'll look after you.

Sean   That should be my job.

Gail   We'll look after each other then. Happy? (*Calls.*) Natalie, dinner! You coming down?

Sean   Gail?

Gail   Oh, remind me after we've eaten, that I need to go on TFL online, I need to work out how to get to Natalie's five-a-side from the station. Where are you coming from?

Sean   Right here I suppose.

Gail   I'll find a route for you as well. Natalie!

Sean   She's asleep.

Gail   She's playing Candy Crush on her phone more like. Natalie?

Sean   She met some girls from across the road today, a couple of sisters, she spent all day hanging out with them.

Gail   Oh, that's it then, she'll be up all night on Snapshot or something. Maybe I should go up.

Sean   Don't embarrass her.

Gail   I'm not. I just want a family dinner.

Sean   And I want us to have some time together.

Gail   Oh, do you now?

Sean   You're up at the crack. You come home late. I've barely seen you all week.

Gail   You just wanted to see me in my uniform again, didn't you? I can read you like a book, Sean Wilde.

Sean   Yeah, I wanted to see you, I wanted to see you get out of that uniform, bit by bit, did you read that part?

They kiss, followed by undressing each other.

There is trouble brewing on the streets. Mixed-raced youths are gathering outside an electrical store.

Gail   Get up those stairs.

Sean   Can I give the orders for once?

Gail   So, give.

Sean   Stairs!

Gail *leads* **Sean** *upstairs.*

Lukas *comes out of his electrical shop waving a baseball bat about in one arm and holding a teenage youth in a headlock in the other. Some of the youths are taunting him.*

Lukas   Come on, you bastards, come on! You want him, come and get him, come on, I fucking dare yer!

Spence, **Gail** *and* **Chris** *are arriving outside the shop.*

Spence   Do you want to put that down, mate?

Lukas   See what am I doing?

Chris   Hard not to from here.

Lukas   Doing your job is what?

Spence   And we appreciate it, don't we, lads?

Chris   Ecstatic.

Lukas   Go find work, the fucking lot of you.

Chris   Oi, language!

Spence   That is no way to speak, now is it?

Lukas   Not you, them!

Spence   We know that.

Lukas   They're the same bastards that tore my shop apart three years ago, do you know that? Now they are trying again, the bastards!

Spence   Maybe, but we need you to put the bat down.

Chris   Lukas, come on, mate!

Lukas *puts down the bat.*

Spence   And him.

Lukas *releases the youth.* **Chris** *takes him.*

Spence   Alright boys, now what's it going to be?

The hoodies huddle up and move a little closer to the police.

Oh, like that, is it?

The hoodies move a lot closer.

Right, so what is this, then? You think you can take what you want, get your mate? You are welcome to try, but we are not backing off this time, so what's it going to be? Just do yourselves a favour and turn around, now!

The youths begin to retreat. **Chris** *ogles* **Gail***'s backside.*

Chris   'Kin 'ell!

Gail   Having fun back there? I can bend down and pretend I'm picking something up if you like?

They all laugh.

One of the youths throws a missile. It misses **Gail***'s head by a good few yards.*

Chris   Motherfucker, hey!

Spence   Leave it. It's what they want, us to go after them. I am not in the mood for it. You alright, Gail?

Gail (*clearly rattled*)   I'm fine, spot on, not a worry.

Spence   Get the word from Lukas. We're going to have a little chat.

He and **Chris** *take the youth aside.*

Spence   So, what do we have there, then?

Chris *searches the youth, finds an iPhone still in the box.*

Chris   Oh, merry Christmas! You have hit the jackpot, haven't yer?

Kid   It's mine.

Chris   What, and still in the box?

Spence (*recognises the* **Kid**)   What are you doing here?

Kid   Say?

Spence   Answer!

Chris   Spence?

Spence   This is the kid I questioned about that gang rape on Kingsley Road the other week. I gave you a chance.

Kid   I know you did. Cheers, blud!

Spence   You want to make jokes?

Chris   Is it a Five?

Kid   What?

Chris   Five!

Spence   Did you not hear what I said?

Chris (*reads the box*)   'iPhone 5'.

Spence   I gave you a chance!

Chris   Five-C in fact.

Spence   Making jokes.

Kid   I dunno.

Chris   Bloody should know. Present and that.

Spence   What do you all call it, 'grafting'?

Chris   Grafting? Wurtless teif you!

Spence   Look at me.

Kid   What you want?

Spence   Respect! Is that too much to bloody well ask?

Kid   I wasn't nicking it – I was going to pay for it.

Chris   With what?

Spence   Oi! I said look at me.

Chris *feels the* **Kid***'s heart.*

Kid   Get off, man.

Chris   Jesus, feel this kid's heart.

Spence *feels the* **Kid***'s heart.*

Spence   Whoa, what you pumping there, oil?

Kid   I'm telling you, I was going to pay, man.

Spence   You are telling me bollocks! What your mates did to that girl, was that bollocks as well?

Kid   You still on that? Fretting over some yat.

Spence   What did you say?

Kid   Wurtless ho was up for it.

Spence   'Wurtless ho'?

Kid   You don't believe? I still got it on my phone, watch.

Spence *grabs the* **Kid** *by the throat.*

Chris   Oh man, just hurry it up.

Spence *slaps the* **Kid** *hard across the head several times. He screams in pain.*

Chris   What you gonna do, call the police? Like you say, they ain't all that!

The coppers continue to beat the **Kid** *until* **Gail** *runs in on them. They stop when they see her.*

Spence   Remember him? You wanna bit? Come on, make it quick!

Gail   I think it's time to leave, don't you?

Chris *and* **Spence** *drag the suspect along.*

Gail *is back at the station.* **Don** *is conversing with* **Spence** *and* **Chris***.*

Gail   Sarge? Sarge?

Don   Just a sec. Straight off, I knew it was going to be bad news, I mean who else call you that early in the morning, from Jamaica?

Spence   Yeah, so?

Don   My dad died.

Spence   Shit.

Chris   Sorry, mate.

Don   For what? He ran out on us when I was three, I grew up thinking he was dead anyway. It turns out, though, the old bastard only left me something in his will. Ten grand. As well as a house, as well as a bar by the sea.

Spence   Nice!

Don   I thought that'd get your cock hard.

Gail   Can I have a word please?

Don (*ignores her*)   They want me to go over and look.

Chris   A bar by the sea? True say, your arse isn't coming back.

Don   Knowing my dad, it will be a shithole.

Chris   You'll follow Maxine out of this, I know it.

Spence   Maxine isn't going anywhere. And neither are you.

Don   Fuck Jamaica. I don't have time for it.

Gail   Look, I saw.

Don   Just hold it in for a sec. (*To* **Spence** *and* **Chris**.) Listen, I may need you boys for a bit of overtime at some point over the next few weeks, you game?

Spence   For what?

Don   Something big, mi tell yu!

Spence (*eager*)   How big?

Don   About nine kilos of smack hidden under some dealer's floorboards. Is that big enough for you?

Spence   Tell me I'm dreaming.

Chris   Damn, Sarge!

Spence   How good is the intel?

Don   Very good. I've been on it for months.

Chris   Fuck, Inspector, they'll make you bleeding Commissioner, cha rass!

Don   So help me out, nuh? Overtime? Bring it home for me.

Spence   Oh, what do you think?

Chris   On it, man!

Don   My boys!

Gail (*given up waiting*)   I would like to make a statement please?

Spence (*to* **Don**)   Have a word, yeah?

Don   I said I will deal with it, now jog on.

Spence *and* **Chris** *go.*

Gail   I bloody well saw them . . .

Don   No, you didn't.

Gail   You don't even know what I'm going to say.

Don   I know. I just don't want to know. Look around. Things go off, on both sides.

Gail   That doesn't make it right.

Don   Listen to you, five minutes here and you think you can give me the arsehole?

Gail   Can I make a statement about what I saw or not?

Don   No, you cannot. You've only been here five minutes, you'll be branded a tell-tale by the whole relief.

Gail   Fuck the relief!

Don   Less of it, Wilde, you haven't earned the right. You're no better than us.

Gail   I know that.

Don   Then save your battles. Trust me, you're going to need them. And don't you ever fucking talk when I am talking. Clear?

Gail *walks into the next scene with* **Sean**.

Gail   Are you going to go on all night about this?

Sean   It's wrong and you know it.

Gail   So now I'm getting a lecture from you, my husband the banker!

Sean   I didn't think you wanted it to be like that.

Gail   I didn't want it to be like that. But I am in the Met now. They just like to do things a little hardcore here.

Sean   A little?

Gail   I'm just saving my battles.

Music playing loudly from upstairs.

Gail   What is this?

Sean (*calls*)   Natalie? Natalie? She's just upset. They lost today, 4–0.

Gail   And what, she's taking it out on me?

Sean   You weren't there. You promised you'd go.

Gail   So she is blaming me? (*Calls.*) Natalie? Have you got something to say to me? Natalie!

Sean   Let me go up.

Gail   I tried my all to get there, what more does she want?

Sean   She understands.

Gail   Do you?

Sean   The Met is hardcore, I get it.

Gail   It's not just that, Sean.

Sean   You wanted to come here.

Gail   I thought *we* wanted to come here.

Sean   Look, let's not have a row about this.

Gail   I'm not having a row, I'm having a talk.

Sean   The builder came to look at the windows today. He's fully booked until the new year. If we want the work done, he says he can fit it next April. Is that alright with you?

Gail   Of course it is.

Sean   I told him you'll give him a ring next week. He'll send you a quote. See what you think.

Gail   Yeah. You just leave it to me.

She walks into the next scene, joining **Spence** *as they respond to a call-out to* **Marcus** *and* **Kristal**.

Marcus   That nosey Asian bitch again.

Gail   Watch your mouth, please?

Marcus   She just can't keep it out.

Gail   Calm down.

Marcus   It was just a silly argument.

Gail   An argument?

Marcus   We have them all the time, you should see what she does to me.

Gail   I'm getting a dash of déjà vu here.

Marcus   Say?

Gail   That's almost exactly what Kristal said.

Marcus   Maybe you should believe her?

Gail   Maybe you should rein your temper in?

Marcus   Maybe!

Gail   Don't you smile at me.

Marcus   Or what?

Gail   Get back.

Marcus   What are you going to do?

Gail   I said get back.

Marcus   Yeah, I know all about that look. Kristal's look, when she's scared.

Gail   Is she in? I would like to see her please?

Marcus (*calls*)   Kristal?

Kristal *appears by the door.*

Gail   How are you doing, Ms Turner?

Marcus (*mocks*)   'Ms Turner'?

Gail   Are you alright?

Spence (*answering a call on his radio*)   456, receiving?

Marcus   She's fine.

Gail   I'm asking her. Kristal?

Kristal   It's nothing.

Spence   Right, on way. Gail?

Gail   Look at me.

Kristal *looks.*

Gail   Has he harmed you?

Spence   Gail?

Gail   Has he threatened you in any way?

Spence   We have to go.

Marcus   Yeah, go.

Spence   There's a brawl going on in the King George pub.

Gail   Kristal?

Kristal   My fault, I walked into a door.

Gail   Kristal, come on.

Kristal   Leave me alone.

She goes back inside.

Gail (*to* **Marcus**)   Take that smile off your face.

Marcus   You go move or what?

Spence (*steps in*)   Marcus Gregory?

Marcus   That's my name, and?

Spence   I wasn't sure but now I know? Angie Gregory's your mum, right? I must have arrested her a dozen times for possession. Likes to bite, we hated going near her.

Marcus   So?

Spence   She was a whore.

Marcus   Come again?

Spence   I said she was a whore. The biggest nastiest dirtiest whore there was. The amount of guys she had digging her out, I've lost count, any moron with a dick.

Marcus   You mind yourself.

Spence   You want take a swing, Marcus? You must want to know what it's like hitting a man.

Gail   Spence?

Spence   You don't tell us to back off, ever. We tell you.

Marcus   So, tell me.

Spence   Step back.

Marcus   You going now?

They go. **Spence** *clocks* **Gail***'s unhappy face.*

Spence   DVs are shit.

Gail   Right now, he's giving her the worst beating she's ever had.

Spence   And if she's got any sense she'll make a complaint, but you know she won't.

Gail   That's not what this is about.

Spence   Have you still got the arsehole about that kid?

Gail   I've got the arsehole because I'm supposed to be helping people.

Spence   But you're not.

Gail   No.

Spence   Welcome aboard. You're a copper now.

A dishevelled-looking man approaches them.

Spence   Yes, mate?

Gail   Can we help you, sir? Sir?

Spence   Can you speak English?

Without any warning, the dishevelled man brings out a sharp carving knife and goes to attack **Gail***, who shrieks and quickly moves aside, exposing* **Spence** *who is the attacked.* **Gail** *shrieks in horror.*

Spence *is able to sound the alarm on his radio before falling to the floor. The man faces* **Gail***, who is in total fear for her life.*

Gail   Please, please don't! Oh please, please, please, I have a little girl.

The dishevelled man stabs her, he is about to stab her again when sounds of sirens are heard in the distance. He runs away. **Gail** *looks down in horror at the sight of her own blood and then at* **Spence***'s bloodied body. She pulls herself together only slightly, but enough to use her radio.*

Gail   This is 274, officers in need of urgent assistance. We're on the corner of Holloway Drive and Chester Road. I repeat, this is 274, officers in need of urgent assistance. (*Screams.*) This is 274!

End of Act One.

Act Two

Gail *watches as several of her colleagues take turns in offering their condolences to* **Maxine**. **Gail** *holds back*. **Don** *comes over*.

Don   Look, a few of us are finishing up over at the pub.

Gail   What you want, my permission?

Don   I wanted to ask you before I forget if you fancied some overtime this weekend? I need some extra bodies for a raid on a dealer's flat on Saturday. Jermaine Thomas, Bare Money Crew. You'll be taking Spence's place.

Gail   TSG are going in, mob handed on the estate?

Don   No, I'm going in mob handed, on the estate, this is my ting! My boys! TSG are along for the ride. I don't care what they say.

Gail   Right.

Don   It's going be wild. If Spence was here, he'd be creaming himself. This one is for him.

Gail   Triffic, great.

Don   Then you'll see some real changes in the nick, my girl, changes for the good. Gonna kick some arse as Inspector, watch mi nuh!

Gail   Well, let's hope so.

Don   So, overtime, want it?

Gail   I can't.

Don   You got to show willing, Gail, that you are a copper through and through. Get your arse back to work.

Gail   Thank you, Dad!

Don   Do you want to come? To the pub?

Gail   Is this you asking?

Don   It's me asking.

Chris *approaches.*

Chris   We're making a move in a sec, Don, you ready?

Don   Yeah, I'm just coming. Gail?

Gail   Gimme a minute.

Chris   Seriously?

Gail   Oh, look at his face, Don – yes, Chris, seriously!

Chris   Fine by me, let's have it.

Don   See you there.

Gail   Yeah, see you there.

Maxine *approaches* **Gail***.*

Maxine   I thought you were still in hospital.

Gail   I have been out two weeks.

Maxine   Are you alright?

Gail   I'm on painkillers, I'll be fine.

Maxine   Well, that's nice, that you're alright.

Gail   How's Jason?

Maxine   I didn't know you knew him.

Gail   I don't. I only just met him today. I'm sorry. Not thinking straight.

Maxine   You are not alone. I am so fucking drunk right now.

Gail   What?

Maxine   I'm off my tits. I have been drinking all day. As soon as I have emptied my glass, someone is filling it for me. Watch.

She quickly downs her drink. She holds her glass up, and like a flash **Chris** *is filling her glass up.*

Maxine   See?

Gail   Perhaps you should sit down.

Maxine   Perhaps.

Neither of them moves.

He forgot my birthday this year. Spence. He could be a useless fucker sometimes.

Gail   I think he knew that.

Maxine   I didn't. I didn't know that he knew I knew that he was a useless fucker. He tried to make it up to me by cooking me a birthday dinner, and going on and on about 'having' an early night. He wasn't subtle, especially when he's a horny one. Have you ever seen a grown man cry when he can't get any pussy? He had veins coming outta his face, throbbing like no one's business. Like a dam waiting to burst. Tears in his eyes, staring at me like I had just shot Bambi in the head. What could I do? Miss out on the only thing he ever got right? And believe me, babe, he got it right, every time. He had a serious cock on him. I'm not lying.

Gail   Right.

Maxine   Thick.

Gail   I heard you.

Maxine   Firm.

Gail   Max?

Maxine   Dinner! Even if his belly was coming out to here. He made me laugh, still reckoning his flabby arse could fit into his size 34 jeans. This was him.

She mimes trying to put on an extremely tight pair of jeans and holding her breath. Howls of laughter from her.

When I got the knock on my door from my Super telling me
Spence was – The first thought that came into my head was
he must have been stabbed in the stomach, because his gut
was always bulging out of his stab vest. 'I lost my voice telling
him to lose weight, the fat useless cunt' – that's what I said.
The Super did not know where to put himself, bless his heart.

There is a moment where neither says anything. **Maxine** *pours more
wine for them.*

Maxine   Talk to me. How is you?

Gail   Just getting by, getting on. Back into the job.

Maxine   Counselling?

Gail   I've had enough counselling. It's not making what
happened go away.

Maxine   Maybe it's not supposed to.

Gail   I didn't do anything wrong, you know.

Maxine   I must have told Spence a million times to get out,
and all I ever got from him was 'Maxine, shut up!' When is
anyone ever going to listen to me?

Gail   Alright.

Maxine   What part of this is alright, Gail?

Gail   I'm sorry.

Maxine   How can you not know what that slag looked like?

Gail   I just can't.

Maxine   He was standing a foot away from you, with a
knife that he shoved right into you.

Gail   It happened so fast.

Maxine   IC1?

Gail   I don't know.

Maxine   IC2?

Gail   I don't know.

Maxine   IC 3, 4, 5, 6!

Gail   You can go through all of the colours in the rainbow Max, I still don't know.

Maxine   Tell me he was wearing a mask at least, give me something, girl, come on.

Gail   He was not wearing a mask,

Maxine   How do you know?

Gail   Because I saw his face.

Maxine   But you don't know what he looked like?

Gail   That's right! God!

Maxine *finishes her drink.* **Chris** *darts over to fill up her glass.*

Maxine   Fuck off, Chris!

Chris *shies away. He re-joins the other officers, including* **Don***, as they usher themselves out of the room.*

Lee *enters, starts to shoot hoops in the background.*

Maxine   I'm going home.

Gail   I'll get your driver.

Maxine   I'll do it. You might forget what he looks like.

Gail   Maxine, please? I'm sorry.

Maxine   I've had enough of people's sorrys! You know what you can do with your bloody sorry! What's the matter with you? I'm going back to an empty house, and everything smells of him, and you can't even remember what the slag looked like?

Gail *downs a couple of pills. She then walks into the next scene.*

Gail *walks up to* **Lee** *and grabs his ball and holds on to it.*

Lee   Yeah, so what do you want?

Gail   You really don't like answering your phone, do you, Lee?

Lee   You don't own me.

Gail   This is your endz, is it not?

Lee   You think it was one of us who done him? Are you mad? A fed getting jooked round here, it's bad for business. Jermaine is pissed about it himself, it weren't us.

Gail   I know that.

Lee   Right, so, we done?

Gail   Not so fast, handsome. Find out for me.

Lee   I swear, you lot are going to dead me before my time.

Gail   What does that mean?

Lee   All last week, yeah, I've had Jermaine asking me questions, troubling me like you are doing right now. What do I know about this fed, why were you always seen with him? Lee, why is it always you he does an SAS on, on and on wid it? If he don't know now I was working with Spence, he soon will if you don't stop troubling me. And when he does, he will light me up like a firework. Money ain't gonna cut it this time.

Gail   So what do you want from me?

Lee   Get him off my back, so he won't suspect me.

Gail   And how am I supposed to do that?

Lee   Be my friend, innit?

Gail   Your friend?

Lee   Keep me in the know.

Gail   What's 'the know', Lee?

Lee   Say for example you give me a heads-up, let me know what you are planning, anything that might help Jermaine.

Gail   Fuck that.

Lee   Come on, girl.

Gail   I'm not your girl.

Lee   Give me one week, and I will have whoever merked Spence signed and sealed for you. But you gotta be my friend first. Come on, Gail, you know it mek sense here.

Gail   You have absolutely no idea what you are asking me to do right now, have you?

Lee   I know exactly what I am asking. If you lot are planning something for Jermaine, I want to know about it. You do, innit? I knew it. Well, let me have it then.

Gail   Back off.

Lee   You want my help, you need to tell me what it is right now, or don't show your face round here again. Make your mind up time.

Gail   Don't you fuck with me.

Lee   Yeah, I know, safe. Well?

Gail   A heads-up?

Lee   Just once in a while.

Gail   You mean if I knew, say, Jermaine's flat was going to get a visit on Saturday, early in the morning? That kind of heads-up?

Lee   Yeah, exactly.

Gail   Well then, I would have to think about it.

Lee   My girl!

Gail   One week!

She throws the ball back.

Lee   A pleasure doing business.

Gail   Lee, just tell me something, yeah, who are we?

Lee   Who are you?

Gail   Us, the uniform, what does it say to you? What do we all look like to the likes of you now?

Lee   You all look fucked.

He goes. **Gail** *joins the next scene, back at the station.* **Don** *enters followed by* **Chris**.

Don   Alright?

Gail   Fine, thanks.

Chris   Jamaica, Don?

Don   Yeah, I know where it is, Chris.

Chris   And it's all yours, the house and the bar?

Don   According to my brief, it's all legit.

Chris   You can swim in the ocean, lie on the beach, look up at the sun and soak it all up, and if you can be bothered in the slightest, think about us poor fuckers still here doing this shit?

Don   That's right.

Chris   And your arse is still here?

Don   Yes, yes, correct!

Chris   You're mad, Don, totally mad.

Don   Shut yer face and get to work.

Chris *goes.* **Don** *sees* **Gail**.

Don   And you are forty seconds late.

Gail   Arrest me.

Don   That was a joke, by the way.

Gail   Was it?

Don   Did you get home alright? From the pub?

Gail Yeah, I got home alright. Look, about last night. I'd rather we just forget about what happened, alright?

Don Is this you not wanting to talk about it?

Gail Talk about what? What did you think happened last night, Don, what did you see? Silk sheets and scented candles? I see the back of my shoulder all bruised from you throwing me against the wall in the gents' loo with your trousers down to your ankles.

Don It was a little bit more than that.

Gail Only in your mind, mate.

Vince *enters.*

Vince Good morning.

Gail What's so fucking good about it?

Don Can we help you with something?

Vince I'm Pennant. Coming over from Vauxhall.

Don We know who you are, Pennant. We've been expecting you.

Vince Call me Vince.

Gail Call him Sarge.

Vince Right, Sarge.

Don Locker room is through there on your right, parade is in ten. Do not be late.

Vince No chance. I'm really glad to be here, Sarge.

Gail You'll learn.

Vince *goes.*

Don I'm not sorry, you know.

Gail I was drunk.

Don So you are saying I took advantage of you?

Gail   Yes, Don, that must be it. I mean as if!

Don   Meaning?

Gail   Well, no offence, but you could fuck a hamster with your dick.

Don   You're going to be late for parade.

Gail   I know.

Don   Get out of my face.

Gail   Watch over the new boy, shall I?

Gail *walks into the next scene. She and* **Vince** *are sitting opposite a battered looking* **Kristal***.*

Kristal   I don't know why she can't leave it alone.

Gail   Who?

Kristal   Who you think? That Asian bit – woman, my neighbour. She has too much to say for her own good.

Gail   He.

Kristal   Say?

Gail   He. Not she. She – Mrs Gupta, the one who cannot stop sticking her nose in – moved out a month ago.

Kristal   Right.

Gail   Marcus going for you again?

Kristal   It's nothing.

Vince   It does not look like nothing.

Kristal   I feel fine.

Gail   Let me guess – your face landed on the cooker?

Kristal   It was an accident.

Gail   Of course it was.

Kristal   Are you saying you don't believe me?

Vince   Kristal, we can help you. You do know that.

Gail   She knows.

Kristal   I don't want help.

Gail   Like I knew she was going to say that.

Kristal   Just let him go.

Gail   Kristal, how long are you going to keep doing this? It's getting boring.

Vince   Easy, Gail.

Kristal   You're the ones bothering me.

Gail   We have him in custody right now. Take the kids, leave the flat, go somewhere!

Kristal   Where?

Gail   A bleeding refuge for a start, Jesus H!

Kristal   He'll find me.

Vince   Not if you make a complaint.

Gail   She won't.

Vince (*surprised*)   What?

Kristal   Who said I won't?

Vince   Don't you want this to stop, Kristal?

Kristal   What do you think?

Gail   Then help yourself.

Vince   Help us to help you. (*Waves a form.*) This is a 124D form.

Gail   She knows what it is.

Vince (*not listening*)   We can go through this, step by step, if that is what you want.

Gail   She knows all this.

Vince   Kristal?

Gail (*growing impatient*)   Kristal! Hello! Is there anybody there?

Vince (*protests*)   PC Wilde!

Gail   You what?

Vince   Kristal?

Kristal   Yeah, yeah, sounds good. I'll think about it.

Vince   You know where we are.

Kristal *goes. Music starts playing.*

Vince   You were a bit strong with her, weren't you?

Gail   I have seen it and heard it all before.

Vince   Yes, but even so –

Gail   Don't finish that sentence. Don't even bother, don't even try.

Vince   We have a job to do, or have you forgotten that?

She walks into the next scene. Her home. Loud music playing from upstairs.

Gail   Will you tell her to turn that shit down?

Sean *enters.*

Gail   Not going to ask where I've been?

Sean   I know where you've been.

Gail   I'm sorry.

Sean   You don't mean it, so don't say it.

Gail   I'm sorry that you had to iron your own bleeding shirt for once.

Sean   Not tonight, Gail.

Gail   Natalie! Turn it down!

The music stops.

Thank fuck! So, what's all that about?

Sean   She says she hates you.

Gail   Yes, of course she does.

Sean   She's fifteen, Gail. Of course she hates you.

Gail   I hate her too, with a passion. (*Sees his face.*) Joke!

Sean   Are you alright?

Gail   Same old same old, really.

Sean   Did you hear my question?

Gail   Did you hear my answer?

Sean *shows her the empty pill bottle.*

Sean   This is empty.

Gail   I can see that. I will have to call for another prescription.

Sean   Look at the date, you were prescribed those two weeks ago. There should be at least half a bottle left. Do you want to talk about it?

Gail   There's nothing to tell.

Sean   Well, in that case, if there is nothing to tell, maybe you wouldn't mind being quite finished for the day acting like you have a dick between your legs.

Gail (*chuckles*)   You don't like being the girl, do you Sean? If I am too much for you, you only have to say. I'll tone it down if you like.

Sean (*clearly rattled*)   Natalie has a boyfriend.

Gail   Since when?

Sean   A couple of weeks.

Gail   This been going on a couple of weeks without you telling me?

Sean   It's nothing, it won't last.

Gail   She's too young to have a boyfriend.

Sean   Well, you talk to her.

Gail   Too fucking right.

Sean   Not like that.

Gail   This wouldn't have happened under my watch. You need to pick up the pace, mate. Why can't you do something for once? Why can't you do anything?

Sean   You are in and out of this house like it's a hotel, popping pills like they are Skittles, and you're barking orders.

Gail   Try going out getting a job, see what it's like?

Sean   Like I can't see already.

Lee *comes on. He is shooting hoops.*

Gail   I can't do everything, Sean.

Sean   No one is asking you to.

Gail   I want to come home to my family without the grief, maybe you could make dinner once in a while, kiss my face, gimme a shag, is that too much to ask?

Sean   I'm here. I could have gone out but I stayed.

Gail   You should have gone.

Sean *(snaps)*   Why don't you go?

Gail *leaves.*

Sean *(calls)*   Yes good, idea.

Lee   Without a doubt!

Sean *leaves.*

Gail *faces* **Lee**.

Lee   You should have seen Jermaine's face when the feds left his yard on Saturday. Grinning from ear to ear.

Gail   I'm very happy for him.

Lee   Him and me are like brothers now.

Gail   Well?

Lee   What you want?

Gail   You said a week.

Lee   I know what I said.

Gail   Do better.

Lee   'S right.

Gail   What was that?

Lee   Nuttin.

Gail   Was that a smirk, Lee?

Lee   What?

Gail   Did you just pull a smirk at me?

Lee   No.

Gail   You did, you bloody smirked at me, didn't you? What is this, a game to you? I did for you, now I expect you to do for me.

Lee   You can expect all you like.

Gail   Don't you fuck with me.

Lee   You are lucky you have that uniform on, cos you would have had a bitch slap this big by now.

Gail   You little shit, you do as I say.

Lee   Move!

Gail   Do you think I won't tell Jermaine about you?

Lee   You won't do that, not unless you want me go barking to the feds about you.

Gail   Little shit.

Lee   Go bark somewhere else.

Gail   Spence helped you.

Lee   Spence helped himself.

Gail   Tell me who killed him!

Lee   What makes you think I know? What makes you think I ever knew? When are you lot going to understand, when are you going to get it, you ain't nothing any more.

Gail *joins* **Kristal**.

Kristal   Right, I'm ready. so where is it?

Gail   Where is what, Kristal?

Kristal   That form you had.

Gail   The form?

Kristal   Don't piss about.

Gail   Oh, you mean the 124D form?

Kristal   Yes, yes, that's the one, are you going to give it to me?

Gail   Are you choosing to make a complaint this time?

Kristal   What do you think? Yes, I am choosing to make a complaint against him, that bastard.

Gail   You don't look injured, do you?

Kristal   What does that matter, pass the form.

Gail   What is this about, Kristal?

Kristal   Him getting off with some ho, that is what it is about. Me. Only finding out, two kids he has with her. Spending my money on his ho and two kids!

Gail   So this time he has not harmed you?

Kristal   Not this time.

Gail   Well, in that case, there is not much we can do.

Kristal   What do you mean? You have seen my face.

Gail   The face you said happened because you fell down the stairs. How many times?

Kristal   I want him put away now, he's been threatening me.

Gail   I'll tell you what. Before we go through this. It will help to make your case stronger if you wait until he assaults you again.

Kristal   Say?

Gail   Get him to assault you.

Kristal   What?

Gail   Get him to give you a beating. Provoke him. Start a fight with him. Tell him he's got a small dick. That you have been cheating on him. Push him to the edge, Kristal, the very edge. As soon as he does, then we'll have him. Then it will be my pleasure to arrest him. An honour even.

Kristal   Are you sure?

Beat. **Gail** *downs some more pills.*

Don *enters.*

Gail   What? Don't look at me like that. Do you know how many times I have had to listen to her excuses for him?

Don   They heard her screaming a street away. When they kicked the door in, they found him using an iron on her. It took six of them to pull him off.

Gail Don't.

Don He caved her head in.

Gail I'm sorry.

Don She's going to be on crutches for the rest of her life.

Gail I said I was sorry but the silly bitch was always going back to him.

Don I know that. Now you have a story to tell. You have seen her before, over and over. She always refused to make a statement. You always tried to persuade her, but she was living in fear of him, blah, blah – Are you listening?

Gail Yes.

Don You don't tell anyone what you said to her.

Gail Alright, can we change the subject here please? How did it go on Saturday, the raid?

Don You didn't hear?

Gail Hear what?

Don Total waste of time, is what. He cleaned his place out, he knew we were coming. So, not only are the Drugs Squad, hopping mad, saying we have a leak, I had fucking Clint going all Jack Bauer on some brer who was mouthing off at him. So bang goes another dream.

Gail Come off it.

Don That was my chance, Gail, and it's gone.

Gail Shut up.

Don You didn't see the look the Super was giving me. Like I was nothing. Like my twenty years in this job mean shit to him. No way are they giving it to me now.

Gail Alright, if that's how you feel, forget it then. The Super is a knob, I've only heard you say it about a million bloody times.

Don   Maybe.

Gail   No maybe about it. Any ideas on who told?

Don *looks at her.*

Vince *enters with a pint in his hand. Clearly drunk.*

Vince   I think I should go home.

Don *leaves.*

Gail   Are you lame or something?

Vince   I wasn't quite planning on staying out this late.

Gail   Well, you are. A new boy always gets smashed after his first week. Peel's tenth point of policing.

Vince   I didn't think you liked me much.

Gail   What, a cutie like you? How could I resist?

Gail *grabs his arse to squeeze.*

Vince   Oi!

Gail   Oi what?

Vince   I was only trying to help. You know, with that girl, Kristal.

Gail   There was no helping her.

Vince   We could have tried though.

Gail   You mean I could? What do you think I had been doing?

Vince   Giving up?

Gail   Oh, so Vinnie boy has some front, eh?

Vince   It's Vince.

Gail   I like it.

Vince   I hate it when people call me Vinnie.

Gail   Keep that up and you and I are definitely going to get along. Give your wife something to really worry about.

Vince   I'm not married.

Gail   Girlfriend?

Vince   What of it?

Gail   You live together?

Vince   Yeah.

Gail   Going well?

Vince   Yeah.

Gail   No burnt dinners then?

Vince   Look, what is this?

Gail   I was only asking if it's going well, what do you think – that I want to jump yer cos you have got a nice arse? Get off your high horse, mate.

Vince   Right. You think it's all pointless, don't you? What we do. Nothing but a LOB.

Gail   I feel a lecture coming on.

Vince   You might be right, in fact, you probably are right. It is a load of bollocks.

Gail   Then why are you grinning?

Vince   Because there will never come a better time for us, Gail.

Gail   English?

Vince   To make things right, to let them know –

Gail   Let me guess, the public?

Vince   What we represent, our values . . . Where we stand!

Gail   Yeah, yeah, yeah, we all want to know where we stand. And you are going to show us the way, aren't you, Moses?

Vince   If I'm up to it.

Gail   Vinnie the fucking saint!

Vince   Vince!

Gail   Vinnie with the values! Vinnie the big man! Is that what it is, Vince, are you the big man? Yeah? Go on, show me.

She grabs his crotch. **Vince** *pushes her off.*

Vince   What the –

Gail   Is this all a bit much for you? Yeah? A bit too fucking intense for you, is it? I don't blame you.

Vince   Look, I really don't know what . . .

Gail   Let me tell you where I stand, yeah? Let me tell you about my *values*. I had to deal with this mugging. Some blonde wannabe-glamour-model MILF was a witness, the very word *stupid* doesn't do her justice. I went round to her house, to get her a statement, no answer. I had a neighbour telling me she took an Easyjet to Ibiza, nice of her to tell us. A couple of weeks later, I go back, she's standing there as brown as Halle Berry. I ask if she's ready to make the statement, she then proceeds to waste half an hour of my life with some shit about have we got the bloke who smashed her mum's kitchen winder? I tried, with all of my will and all of my power, to get a word in, explaining that is not my case. And then trying to convince her it wasn't me that her thick as shit mother made the complaint to. I goes, 'Was the person driving a car that said Police on the side?' She said, 'Yes, how did you know?' So, that was it. I took a deep breath, picked up a carving knife and stabbed her repeatedly in the neck with it. I've got her buried underneath the floorboards in my house. Stinks the whole place out something rotten. What? It had to be done. People like that, are just too stupid to live. That's where I stand, Vinnie.

Vince   Right. OK, that's it, I'm gone.

Gail   No, you're not fucking gone. You're not fucking gone at all.

She clumsily attempts to pull **Vince** *towards her in order to kiss him. He pushes her off.*

Vince   I'm going home now.

Gail   Finish your fucking drink, you cunt.

She pours the drink over him.

Sean *enters.*

Gail   Just kiss me.

Loud music playing from upstairs.

Gail (*covers her ears*)   Oh, what is this?

Sean   You missed another game.

Gail   And you both have the arsehole about it, yes? Thank you!

Sean   She scored two goals, two beautiful goals that will stay with me for the rest of my life. What have you got, Gail? What have you done today?

Vince *leaves.*

Gail   Apart from working a ten-hour shift that's going to keep a roof over our heads until that glorious day when you actually get a job?

Sean   What are you doing?

Gail   Trying to shag you is what I am doing. Or do I have to iron all of your shirts and make you something to eat first? Natalie, turn that shit down!

Sean   You stink of drink.

Gail   I tell you, Sean, sometimes I have wondered if you bat for the other team.

Sean   Get away from me.

Gail   Sean, please, I'm not fucking joking. Don't make me have to give you a fucking order.

Sean   An order?

Gail   You can be the big man again tomorrow, but right now I am telling you to fuck me.

Sean   I'm sick and tired of you telling me.

Gail   Go on. Fuck me.

Sean   I have had it.

Gail (*screams*)   Natalie!

Sean   Just leave her alone, you'll make it worse.

Gail   Come down here.

Sean   That won't help.

Gail   This will.

Gail *kisses him, then suddenly grabs his wrist.*

Sean   Gail, what are you doing?

Gail   We need some order in this house, some respect!

She handcuffs him the door.

Sean   Gail, for Christ sake!

Gail   Where's your baseball bat? In the closet, yeah?

Sean   Gail, I mean it, don't do this.

Gail   My head is thumping here.

Gail *goes out.*

Sean (*yells*)   Gail!

Gail *is offstage smashing her daughter's computer to bits. Her daughter is screaming at* **Gail** *to stop.* **Gail** *comes back in to the living room, the*

sound of her daughter, now weeping, behind her. **Gail** *takes the cuffs off*
Sean.

Sounds of rioting from the streets outside.

Gail   Your little girl wants you.

Sean   I want a divorce. I want a divorce.

Gail   No need to say it twice.

There is pandemonium on the streets. Youths rioting, looting shops. **Gail**
and **Vince** *join* **Don**, **Chris** *and a couple of officers as they all
change into riot gear.*

Don (*recites*)   'Dear Sergeant Walters, in spite of your
excellent service record . . . we regret to inform you . . . ' Oh,
what's the fucking point?

Gail   Maybe you should forget it.

Don   Forget it?

Gail   It weren't to be.

Chris   What she say?

Don   Is that right? Weren't meant to be?

Chris   Shouldn't listen to her.

Gail   Fuck off, Chris.

Don   Nuh, she's right, Chris. It weren't meant to be. I mean,
what is twenty years of service, eh? Well, fuck this job. Fuck it.
As soon as we've cleared this mess up, I'm getting on a plane,
going to Jamaica, live in my dad's house. I gone!

Chris   You said it was a shithole.

Don   It's better than here. Oh Lawd, just let find this
grassing cunt and kill him.

Gail   You've gone through nearly every copper in the
station, you are never going to find him.

Chris   I love how you think he's a he.

Gail   Back off, Chris.

Chris   How do we know it weren't you? I mean, you're not exactly the most reliable copper around, are you?

Gail   What have you got your little cock in a twist about this time, I wonder?

Chris   You're asking what my problem is?

Gail   I liked you better when you had your eyes all over my arse.

Chris   Oh, I can do worse things to your arse than eyeing it up, Wildefire!

Gail   Is that right, big man?

Chris   You only knew Spence, but I loved him, alright?

Gail   Is this you coming out, Chris?

Chris   Useless bitch.

Gail   Any more?

Chris   You should have had his back. That is what you do. It's what I would have done.

Don   Enough. Not now. We have work to do. What are you all waiting for, rain? Let's move!

The officers move out. **Gail** *takes a few painkillers before getting ready to leave.*

Don   You still taking that shit?

Gail   Doctor's orders. You got a problem with that?

Don (*grabs her arm*)   Why are you lying to me?

Gail   Let go of my arm, Don.

They all walk into the next scene. It is carnage everywhere. Teens are looting and rioting. **Don** *instructs the entire relief to form a line.*

Chris Jesus!

A **Senior Officer** *arrives.*

Officer Where's your guvnor?

Don That's me. Yes, sir?

Officer Right, listen up. I've got your people here, plus another three units on its way with any luck. Those lot, come no further! Their fun and games end here! Do not engage!

Vince We're not even going to try?

Officer No, we are not going to try. But if they fancy their chances, drop them by all means. But they will come to us, and we will let them.

Gail This is a joke.

Officer We are outnumbered. And stretched. We go steaming in, these streets are going to burn.

Gail They're burning now.

Don Gail!

Officer Your priority is to protect those two fire crews. You will not leave them, are we clear on that?

Don With all due respect, mate?

Officer What is it, and it's 'sir'!

Don It's only us here, we are not enough to cover two fire crews!

Officer Are you hard of hearing, Sergeant? I said we have reinforcements coming in.

Don We are the reinforcements!

Officer I don't want to hear about it.

Don That is because you are a prick.

Chris   Oh, gosh!

Officer   I beg your pardon?

Don (*louder*)   That is because you are a prick, sir.

Chris   Skipper's gone!

Officer   You picked the wrong night to lose it, Sergeant!

Don   Like I give a rass.

Officer   Are you going to follow orders or not?

Don (*to his officers*)   Come on, you heard the man!

Officer   I am not going to forget this.

Don   Piss off.

The **Officer** *goes.*

Don   Fucking this, fucking job! (*To the officers.*) Come on, let's do this.

The officers hold the line as they are pelted with rocks.

Vince   Oh, Jesus!

Don   Come on, that was nothing.

More missiles are landing on them.

Gail   Oh, this is off!

Don   Come on, hold the line.

Gail   Let's just have them.

Don   This is not a democracy. Come on, hold it together.

Vince   Easier said.

Gail   Mouthy shits, come on!

Chris   Just stay with me, Vinnie, boy!

Vince   It's Vince!

Chris   Who gives a rass, hold the line.

Gail   Right, come on then, ten things you should never say to a copper?

Don   Not now, Gail.

Gail   Ten things you should never say to a copper, come on! I'll start. 'Does your head really fit that hat?' 'Why don't you go and arrest a real criminal?' 'You planted that on me.' 'Have you got a warrant?'

Don   Gail?

Gail   'Am I bovvered?' 'No, I didn't know fast I was going.'

The youths are throwing more missiles.

Gail   'Couldn't you get a job at Burger King? 'How much you want? 'You cunts ain't nothing! 'You on the take or what?

*A missile nearly lands on **Gail**.*

Don   Gail, don't.

*The rioter removes his hood, but only **Gail** sees it. She recognises him straight away as the man who killed **Spence**.*

Gail   You! Fucking you!

Don   Gail!

Gail *breaks the line to chase the rioter.*

Don   Gail, get back! Come back, I said!

Vince *runs to follow **Gail**.*

Don   Vince!

Vince   Can't hear yer, Sarge!

Don   Christ!

*Lights on **Gail**, wrestling with a masked rioter.*

Gail   Show me your face again. Show me, you bastard!

Gail *manages to pull the mask off. She is shocked to see that is* **Maxine**.

Gail   Max? Max, what the fuck, girl? What are you doing? Max?

Maxine *remains silent.* **Gail** *senses something is not right. Another masked rioter approaches.*

Gail   What? What?

She pulls the mask off the rioter: it is **Spence**.

Gail   No, no, no, fuck right off, no!

Two more rioters appears. **Gail** *does the same thing and pulls their masks off. It is* **Sean** *and then* **Kristal**.

Gail (*to them*)   What? What? Well? Say what you have to say, come on.

The four huddle together. They take a few small steps towards her.

Gail   Stand back.

The four edge a little closer.

I won't say it again, stand back.

The four move in closer.

Stand back!

Vince *arrives. He does not see the four. He runs up behind her.*

Vince   Gail?

Gail *jumps, spins around, beats* **Vince** *repeatedly with her baton.*

Vince (*screaming and defending himself*)   It's me, it's me!

Gail *stops.*

Gail   What the fuck are you doing here?

Vince   To help you. Fuck, what is the matter with you?

Don *and* **Chris** *arrive.*

Vince What are you doing? What is going on in that head?

Don Pennant! (*Sees* **Vince**'s *face.*) Oh, Jesus!

Chris I'll get first aid.

Vince Is this what you call policing, is this protecting the public?

Gail Get away from me.

Vince You're no copper.

Don Oi, oi, just take it easy, alright, relax. Gail?

Vince You're a disgrace.

He goes to leave.

Don Where are you going? Pennant, come back here! (*To* **Gail**.) It was you, wasn't it? You told them about the warrant, didn't you? Jesus, Gail. You want to tell me why?

Gail It was the only way.

Don Way? What fucking way?

Gail I was trying to get to Spence's killer.

Don What the hell does that –

Gail Spence had a chis, I was working with him.

Don You were dealing with a chis?

Gail He said he knew.

Don Without telling me, are you stupid?

Gail He said he'd help me get him.

Don And did you, did you get Spence's killer? Of course you fucking didn't.

Gail I had to.

Don You had to? You had to betray the uniform?

Gail Yes, I did!

Don   You need to turn it in, the job. Right now.

Gail   I heard you!

Don   You are done, PC Wilde. You're done.

He goes. **Chris** *arrives with bandages. He sees that everyone apart from* **Gail** *has gone.*

Chris (*to* **Gail**)   What are you like?

Gail *brushes past him as she leaves.*

Kristal *enters, walking on crutches, clutching a child's painting.* **Gail** *enters, now dressed in civilian clothes.*

Gail   He is quite the drawer, your youngest, isn't he? He's getting better and better I think. I could be wrong but I think in this one, that's supposed to be you. And I'm guessing that is supposed to be his sister? He likes his big happy faces, doesn't he? You've got a Picasso in waiting right there, Kristal.

Kristal *is struggling to speak.*

Gail   It's alright, you don't have to speak, just nod. It's OK.

Kristal   How?

Gail   Kids? Sorry, I don't understand?

Kristal   Kids?

Gail   Oh, you mean how they are? They're fine. They miss you, of course, but they are doing alright. It's a really good foster home. They're been well looked after. You won't know, but I brought them round to see you a couple of weeks back, when you were . . . . I didn't think I should, I wasn't going to at first, but your eldest – the mouth on her. She wouldn't give it a rest until I brought them round. She really loves you. They both do. I'll bring them round again if you like, now that you're up.

Kristal *nods. They both sit in silence for a moment.*

Gail   Oh, by the way, I went to look at that shelter up in North London, you know the one with the garden I told you about. It looks alright to me. I'll drive you all there if you want.

Kristal   What?

Gail   Sorry, I don't . . .

Kristal   What you?

Gail   What you?

Kristal   Want?

Gail   What do I want?

Kristal *nods.*

Gail   I was hoping you were never going to ask me that. I suppose right now, at this precise moment, I want to know what is that big hulking four-legged thing that is standing at the back of your son's painting. Do you see it? Do you see it, it's hard to miss. Every painting he has done, no matter what, there it is, that thing. I ask him what it is all the time, he just shakes his head. He's not much of a talker your boy, is he?

Kristal   Ele . . .

Gail   Sorry, what?

Kristal   Ele . . . phant.

Gail   It's an elephant?

Kristal   He likes elephants.

Gail   An elephant it is then.

She is distracted momentarily by the sound of a police car wailing its siren loudly as it whizzes by.

Kristal *tries to pour herself a glass of water, but is struggling with holding the glass.* **Gail** *focuses all of her attention on* **Kristal** *and pours a glass for her, then helps her drink it by raising it to her mouth.*

Gail   How's that?

Kristal *again attempt to speak.*

Kristal (*lets it out*)   Thank you.

Gail *does not answer. She just smiles as she helps* **Kristal** *drink the rest of the water.*

Blackout as the police siren begins to fade.

DRAMA ONLINE

A new way to study drama

From curriculum classics
to contemporary writing
Accompanied by
theory and practice

Discover. Read. Study. Perform.

Find out more:
www.dramaonlinelibrary.com

 BLOOMSBURY *methuen* **drama** 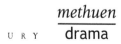 THE ARDEN SHAKESPEARE  **ff** FABER DIGITAL

Bloomsbury Methuen Drama Modern Plays
include work by

Bola Agbaje
Edward Albee
Davey Anderson
Jean Anouilh
John Arden
Peter Barnes
Sebastian Barry
Alistair Beaton
Brendan Behan
Edward Bond
William Boyd
Bertolt Brecht
Howard Brenton
Amelia Bullmore
Anthony Burgess
Leo Butler
Jim Cartwright
Lolita Chakrabarti
Caryl Churchill
Lucinda Coxon
Curious Directive
Nick Darke
Shelagh Delaney
Ishy Din
Claire Dowie
David Edgar
David Eldridge
Dario Fo
Michael Frayn
John Godber
Paul Godfrey
James Graham
David Greig
John Guare
Mark Haddon
Peter Handke
David Harrower
Jonathan Harvey
Iain Heggie

Robert Holman
Caroline Horton
Terry Johnson
Sarah Kane
Barrie Keeffe
Doug Lucie
Anders Lustgarten
David Mamet
Patrick Marber
Martin McDonagh
Arthur Miller
D. C. Moore
Tom Murphy
Phyllis Nagy
Anthony Neilson
Peter Nichols
Joe Orton
Joe Penhall
Luigi Pirandello
Stephen Poliakoff
Lucy Prebble
Peter Quilter
Mark Ravenhill
Philip Ridley
Willy Russell
Jean-Paul Sartre
Sam Shepard
Martin Sherman
Wole Soyinka
Simon Stephens
Peter Straughan
Kate Tempest
Theatre Workshop
Judy Upton
Timberlake Wertenbaker
Roy Williams
Snoo Wilson
Frances Ya-Chu Cowhig
Benjamin Zephaniah

For a complete listing of Bloomsbury
Methuen Drama titles, visit:

www.bloomsbury.com/drama

Follow us on Twitter and keep up to date
with our news and publications

@MethuenDrama

9 781474 236119